Cowboy
Things to Make and Do

Emily Bone

Designed and illustrated by Erica Harrison

Additional illustrations by Vicky Arrowsmith,
Stella Baggott and Josephine Thompson
Steps illustrated by Molly Sage

Edited by Leonie Pratt

Photographs by Howard Allman

Contents

Wild West 'WANTED' poster

If you don't have a digital photo, you could glue a photograph of yourself onto the paper after step 4.

1. Print a black and white digital photo of yourself onto white paper. Tear strips from the edges of the paper. Then, crumple it up and carefully open it out again.

Very carefully, stir the mixture so that the water turns dark brown.

2. To stain the paper, put four teabags into a container. Boil water in a kettle, then very carefully pour the water over the tea bags. Leave the tea to cool.

3. Lay the paper in a wide, shallow dish. Pour the cold tea over the paper so that the paper is completely covered. Then, remove the tea bags.

4. Leave the paper to soak for at least an hour. Then, take the paper out of the tea and lay it on a piece of plastic foodwrap until it is dry.

5. Write 'WANTED' at the top of your poster and an outlaw name underneath. Below your photo, write 'Reward' and '$150,000'. Fill in the words using a felt-tip pen.

WANTED

WANTED
DEAD OR ALIVE

Horse Rustler Hank
$100 000

REWARD
$100 000

You could put on an outlaw outfit then take a photo for your poster.

WANTED
Buffalo Bob
Reward
$150 000

Buffalo Bob
Reward

6. To make yourself look like a Wild West outlaw, draw a cowboy hat on a piece of brown paper. Cut it out, then glue it onto your photo, like this.

7. Draw a bandana on patterned paper. Cut it out and glue it onto the neck. Then, cut out drooping whiskers from black paper and glue them onto the face.

Line dancing paperchain

Leave room for a hat.

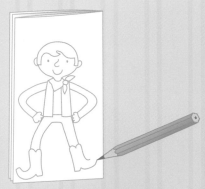

1. Fold a long rectangle of paper in half. Then, fold it in half again. Draw a cowboy's head near the top of the paper and add hair and a face.

2. Draw a body below the head. Then, draw bent arms and hands on either side of the body so that the elbows almost touch the folds, like this.

3. Add clothes on the cowboy. Then, draw legs below the body. Draw boots, making sure that you draw the toes near to the folds on both sides.

Don't cut around the folds, marked here in red.

4. Draw a big brim for a hat around the cowboy's head, so that the sides are close to the edges of the paper. Then, add the top of the hat.

5. Draw a line around the cowboy touching the edges of the paper by the hat, elbows and toes. Cut around the line, through all the layers.

6. Unfold the layers of paper to make a chain. Draw three more cowboys inside the other shapes. Then, fill in all the cowboys using felt-tip pens.

On the range picture

1. Using a black pen, draw a cowboy's head on a piece of white paper. Draw a body and add two arms and hands. Then, draw two legs below the body.

Use the ideas on these pages to add more things such as a town, a lake and more cowboys to your picture.

Leave a space between the cowboy and the horse.

2. Draw a hat on top of the head and add boots at the bottom of the legs. Draw a belt and bandana, then fill in the cowboy and draw the face.

3. Draw a tent on some paper and cut it out. Glue it a little way away from the cowboy. Then, use a black pen to draw lines for the tent flaps and ropes.

4. Draw a horse's body and head using a felt-tip pen. Then, draw ears, a neck and four legs. Fill in the horse. Then, use a black pen to add an eye, mane and tail.

Draw lines between the horse and the wagons.

5. For wagons, cut out two rectangles from paper. Then, cut out four thin strips and glue them onto the wagons. Trim the strips to fit the wagons.

6. Cut the ends of the wagons to make them curved and glue them behind the horse. Cut out four wheels and glue them on, then draw lines for spokes.

7. Cut trees from paper and glue them on. Then, cut out flames and glue them next to the cowboy. Draw the wood below the fire using a thin black pen.

Sheriff collage

'Bowed' legs curve out, like this.

1. Draw a cowboy's bowed legs on a picture of blue jeans from an old magazine. Cut out the legs and glue them near the bottom of a piece of paper.

2. Draw two cowboy boots on brown paper and cut them out. Draw a shirt and cut it out, too. Then, glue the shapes onto the paper, like this.

3. Cut out two rectangles and glue them onto the shirt, like this. Draw a star-shaped sheriff's badge on yellow paper. Cut it out and glue it onto the cowboy's body.

Glue the cuffs where the hands overlap the sleeves.

4. Draw two hands as if they are about to grab something. Cut them out and glue them onto the arms. Then, cut out cuffs and glue them onto the hands.

5. Cut out a head, nose and white circles for eyes, then glue them on. Cut out some hair and glue it onto the cowboy's head. Then, cut out a hat and glue it on, too.

6. Cut two holsters from paper and glue them onto the jeans. Then, use a black pen to draw eyebrows, a mouth and dots in the cowboy's eyes.

To make a showdown scene like this one, make a background from paper first, then glue on two cowboys – a sheriff and an outlaw.

This cowboy's shirt was cut from a picture of a shirt in a magazine.

Cowboy sunset painting

1. To make a sunset sky, pour some thick yellow paint onto an old plate. Then, pour thick orange and red paints onto the plate, too. Spread them out a little.

2. Dip a large paintbrush into the yellow paint. Then, paint a thick strip at the bottom of a white piece of paper, covering about half of the page.

3. Without washing your brush, dip it into the orange paint. Then, paint a thinner orange strip so that it blends into the yellow paint, like this.

4. Paint the top part of the paper red in the same way. When the paint is completely dry, use a pencil to draw a line across the paper for the horizon.

5. For a rearing horse, draw a large, slanting oval for the body above the horizon, like this. Then, draw a smaller oval for the head and a shape for the nose.

6. Add ears on the horse's head and two curved lines for the neck. Then, draw two legs at the back of the horse that go down to the horizon.

7. Draw two bent legs at the front of the horse. Then, draw a mane and a tail. Draw a cowboy's body on the back of the horse, then add the head with a large open mouth.

8. Draw a hat on top of the head, then draw a triangle for the cowboy's nose and add some hair. Draw a pointed boot under the horse's body.

9. Add a curved arm behind the cowboy and one touching the horse's neck. Use thick black paint to fill in the horse, cowboy and area below the horizon.

You could make your picture look like a Wild West desert by drawing rocks and cacti on the horizon.

Fingerprinted ponies

1. Spread thick paint on an old plate. Dip your finger in the paint. Press your finger onto some paper and move it around to fingerpaint two ovals for a horse's body.

2. Dip your finger into the paint again and print a small circle for the head. Then, use your little finger to print a nose. Use a brush to paint the horse's neck and ears.

3. For the horse's legs, cut a small rectangle from thick cardboard. Dip one of the long sides into the paint, then press it onto the paper to print four legs.

4. Leave the paint to dry. To print a cowboy on the horse, dip one short end of the cardboard rectangle in blue paint. Drag it across the paper to make a body.

5. Use the other short side to print the top of the cowboy's leg slanting away from the body. Then, print the bottom half of the leg going the other way.

6. Dip your finger in paint and print the cowboy's head. Leave the paint to dry. Then, draw a face and ears on the cowboy using a thin black pen.

7. Draw the cowboy's arm, then add a hat, scarf and boot. Draw the horse's face, mane and tail. Then, add hooves and a bridle and saddle.

You could use the short end of the cardboard to print a horse with a bending leg.

For a horse from the front or back, print one oval for the body.

Stand-up cattle

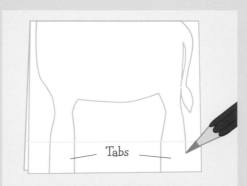

Tabs

1. Fold a rectangle of thick white paper in half. Fold up the ends of the paper to make flaps. They will be the base of the cow. Then, unfold the flaps.

2. Draw a cow's body on the folded paper, so that its back goes along the fold. Add lines coming down from the legs to the bottom of the flaps to make tabs.

3. Draw a cow's head on another piece of thick paper. Add horns, ears and a face. Then, fill in the head and make patches on the body using felt-tip pens.

This cowboy was made with the top of his hat along the fold and the tabs below his heels.

Cut around
the tabs.

4. Cut out the head. Then, keeping the paper folded, cut out the cow's body, through both layers of paper. Don't cut along the cow's back.

5. For the base, fold the tabs under the body. Then, glue one tab on top of the other, like this. Press the tabs together until the glue sticks.

6. To attach the head, cut out a small square from thick cardboard and glue it onto the body, near the front. Glue the head onto the cardboard.

Don't cut along the fold.

7. For a cactus, fold a piece of green paper in half and make flaps, as you did in step 1. Then, draw a long, thin arch so that the top touches the fold.

8. Add branches on either side of the arch. Then, draw around the cactus with a green pen and add stripes. Hold the layers together and cut out the shape.

9. Fold both the tabs under the cactus. Then, glue one tab on top of the other one to make the base. This means that the cactus stands upright.

You could make a herd of cattle and lots more cacti.

Painted cowboy boots

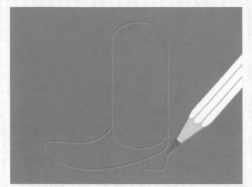  

1. For the leg of the boot, draw a long rectangle with curved ends. Draw a curved line for the toe of the boot. Then, add a small shape for the heel.

2. Fill in the boot using thick paint. Then, while the paint is still wet, use a blunt pencil to scrape swirly patterns on the boot, like this.

3. When the paint is dry, use thick black paint to add a sole and fill in the heel. Then, draw a star for a spur on the back of the boot using a silver pen.

You could copy some of the swirly shapes on these boots.

Sheriff badge

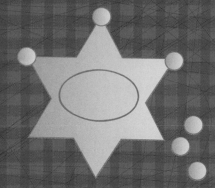

1. Draw a triangle on a piece of thin cardboard. Then, draw an upside-down triangle overlapping the first one to make a star. Cut out the shape.

2. Spread glue on the front of the star and lay it sticky-side down on some kitchen foil. Cut around the star leaving a border, then fold the foil over the edges.

3. Cut an oval and six small circles from cardboard. Cover them with foil. Then, glue the oval onto the middle of the star, and the circles onto the points.

4. Press the tip of a blunt pencil into the foil to make a dotted pattern around the badge. Then, write the word 'SHERIFF' across the oval in the middle.

5. Turn the badge over. Open a paperclip out a little, then, tape one side of it to the back of the badge, like this. Hook the paperclip onto your clothes.

You could make a deputy's badge.

To make a gold badge like the one above, use the foil from a chocolate wrapper.

Saloon door card

These flaps will make the saloon doors.

1. Bend a rectangle of thick brown paper in half and pinch the middle. Lay it flat, then fold over each end to meet the pinch. Crease the folds well.

2. Draw a curved line for the top of a door about halfway up one of the flaps. Then, draw another door on the other flap. Make sure the doors are level on each flap.

3. Cut down the creases on both flaps. Then, carefully cut along the top of both of the doors so that you cut off the section above the lines.

Write your message on the back of the saloon doors.

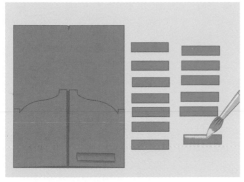

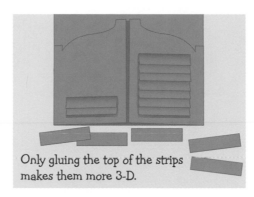

Draw the cowboy's head at the top of the rectangle.

4. Cut a long, thin strip from brown paper and cut it into little pieces. Brush white glue along the top of one piece and glue it near the bottom of one door.

5. Brush a line of glue across the top of another piece and glue it above the first one, overlapping it slightly. Glue the pieces on both doors, like this.

Only gluing the top of the strips makes them more 3-D.

6. Lay the card on a piece of white paper and draw around it. Cut out the rectangle. Then, draw a cowboy's head and add a face and hat.

7. Draw the cowboy's body and legs. Then, add a shirt, bandana, belt and boots. Paint the cowboy using thick paint, then paint the background black.

Glue the card along the bottom of the larger piece of cardboard.

8. When the paint is dry, open the doors and glue the paper onto the card. Then, glue the card onto a bigger piece of cardboard. Cut around it to make a doorframe.

Cowboy hat

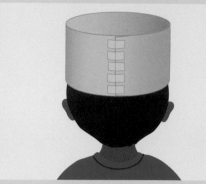

1. To make the hat band, cut a wide strip of thin cardboard that is long enough to fit around your head with a little overlap. Then, tape the ends to secure them.

Hold the band as you draw.

2. Take the band off your head, then gently press the sides together a little to make an oval. Place it on some thin cardboard and draw around it.

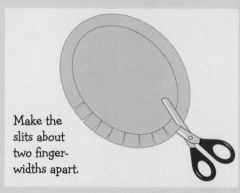

Make the slits about two finger-widths apart.

3. Draw a bigger oval around the first one. Then, cut around the bigger oval. Make flaps by cutting lots of slits in from the edge of the cardboard to the smaller oval.

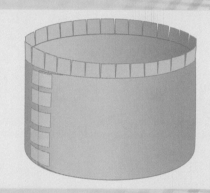

4. Fold up the flaps around the edge of the oval. Then, gently slot the oval inside the hat band, making sure that all the flaps are pointing up.

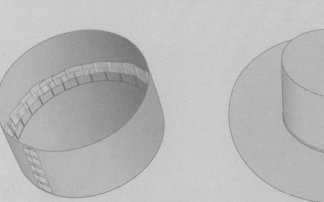

5. Carefully push the oval down into the hat band, all the way to the bottom. Use lots of pieces of sticky tape to secure all of the flaps.

6. For the brim, cut out a big circle from cardboard. Place the hat band in the middle of the circle and draw around it. Then, lift it off.

7. Draw a smaller oval inside the one you have just drawn. Then, gently bend the cardboard in half and hold it in the middle. Cut around the smaller oval.

8. Make flaps by cutting slits all the way around the inside of the brim, up to the line of the bigger oval you drew in step 6. Then, fold all the flaps over.

9. To attach the brim, lay the hat band upside down. Then, slot the flaps on the brim into the hat band. Tape the flaps to the inside of the band.

10. Turn the hat the correct way up. Cut a long piece of ribbon and tie it around the hat band. Then, bend the opposite sides of the brim up, like this.

Cowboy belt

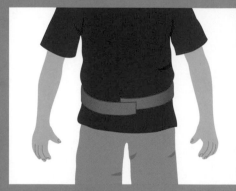

1. To make a belt, cut out a long strip of thin brown cardboard. The belt should be long enough to fit around your hips with a little overlap.

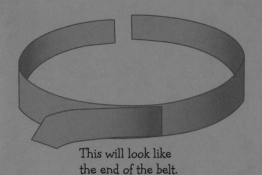

This will look like the end of the belt.

2. Cut another shorter strip that is the same width as the belt. Cut off the corners from one end to make a point. Then, glue the other end onto the middle of the belt.

You could glue on more tiny circles for extra decoration.

3. For a buckle, cut an oval from cardboard. Then, cut out a small circle and a star. Glue the circle in the middle of the oval, then glue the star onto the circle.

4. Cut a piece of string that fits around the buckle. Glue the string just inside the edge of the buckle. When the glue is dry, paint the buckle gold.

Don't cover this end.

5. When the paint is dry, spread glue over the back of the buckle. Then, press it onto the middle of the belt, covering the end of the strip you glued on earlier.

Glue the loop so it looks like it is holding the end of the belt in place.

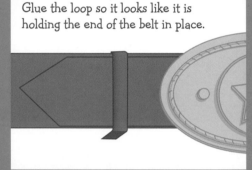

6. Cut a thin strip from cardboard for a belt loop. Lay the strip a little way away from the buckle, then fold the ends around and glue them onto the back of the belt.

Don't cut along the fold.

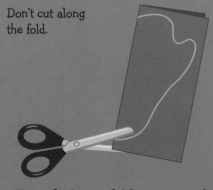

7. For a holster, fold a rectangle of thick paper in half. Then, draw a holster against the fold, like this. Keeping the paper folded, cut out the shape.

Spread glue from here...

...to here.

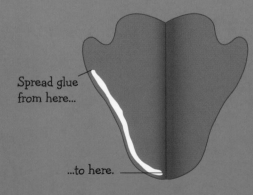

8. Open the holster. Then, spread a line of glue along one of the edges, down to the fold. Fold the holster again and carefully press the edges together.

9. Cut a thin paper strip with curved ends and fold it over the top of the holster. Then, glue one end onto the back of the holster and one onto the front.

Use the ideas on this page to make belts with different buckles.

Glue the holster on this side of the buckle.

Slot it so that the ends are inside the belt.

10. Glue the holster onto the belt. Then, use a brown felt-tip pen to draw patterns and stitching on the holster and belt. Add studs and metal details with a gold pen.

11. Make a cut halfway down into the belt at one end. Then, make a cut going halfway up into the belt at the other end. Slot the ends together to fasten the belt.

Printed rattlesnakes

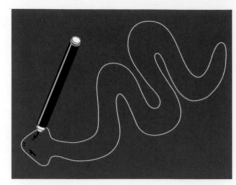

1. Using a pencil, draw a long, wiggly snake's body on red paper and add a triangular head. Then, draw eyes and nostrils with a thin black pen.

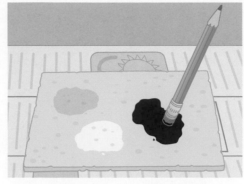

2. Put a kitchen sponge cloth on newspaper. Pour blobs of black, gold and yellow paint onto it. Then, press the eraser on the end of a pencil into the black paint.

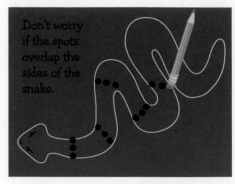

Don't worry if the spots overlap the sides of the snake.

3. Press the eraser onto the snake to print spots. Wiggle the pencil a little as you print to make a bigger spot. Dip the eraser in the paint each time you print.

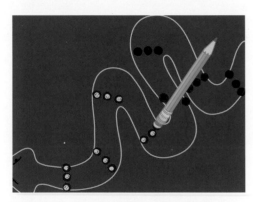

4. Wash the black paint off the eraser. When the spots are dry, dip the eraser into the gold paint and lightly press it onto all of the black circles.

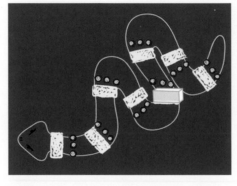

5. For stripes, dip the thin side of an eraser into the yellow paint. Then, press the eraser onto the snake, next to the printed circles, to make stripes.

You could add a snake's tongue cut from pink paper.

6. When the paint is dry, cut out the snake and glue it onto another piece of paper. Draw a rattle on a piece of paper and cut it out. Then, glue it onto the tail.

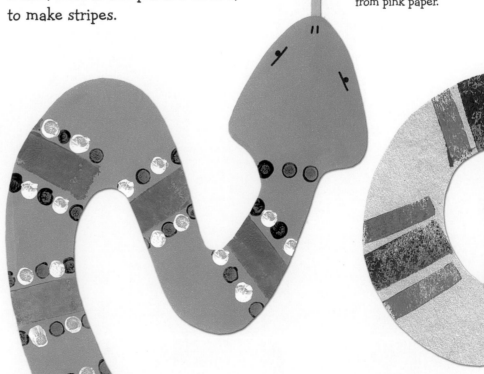

Rattlesnakes live in hot deserts. When they are threatened, they shake their tail, making a sound like a baby's rattle.

Try printing with the thick side of an eraser to make bigger stripes.

Wild West town painting

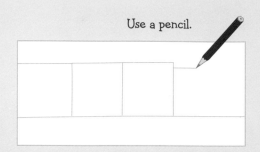

Use a pencil.

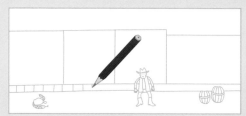

Leave a space here.

1. Draw a line all the way across a piece of thick paper, about a quarter of the way up. Then, draw four buildings above the line, like this.

2. Draw a sheriff, two barrels, some rocks and a snake in front of the buildings. Draw a walkway below the buildings, then add lines for boards.

3. To make a building into a jail, draw a door. Then, draw rectangles on either side of the door for windows and add crossing lines for bars.

Use the ideas on this page for buildings to draw in your town.

4. Draw a balcony halfway up the jail and add two poles down to the walkway. Then, draw four small windows with shutters above the balcony.

5. Add a star between the middle windows and a large sign above. Write the word 'JAIL' on the sign. Then, draw a prisoner looking out of one of the windows.

6. Draw the rest of the buildings. Then, fill in your picture using watery paints. When the paint is dry, go over all the lines using a thin black pen.

Dancing cowboy

1. For a cowboy's head, draw a circle near the top of a piece of thin cardboard. Draw a hat on top of the head, then draw ears and a face.

The holes should go here.

2. Draw the body and arms, then add clothes. Fill in the cowboy and cut out the shape. Then, use a hole puncher to make two holes at the bottom of the body.

As you pull the thread the cowboy's legs will swing up.

Make the top of the legs extra long because the holes will go behind the cowboy's body.

You only need half of the pipe cleaner.

3. Cut two cardboard strips. Punch two holes in the top of each strip. Then, draw the cowboy's legs around the holes, like this. Fill in the legs and cut them out.

4. Cut a pipe cleaner in half, then in half again. Fold two short pieces in half and twist them together. Then, open out the ends of each piece.

5. Turn the cowboy over and line up the bottom hole on one of the legs with one of the holes on the cowboy's body. Push the pipe cleaner through the hole.

28

You could make a cowgirl with long hair, or a cowboy holding his hat.

Don't tie the loop too tight.

6. Lay the cowboy on a flat surface. Gently twist the end of the pipe cleaner down into a knot to secure it. Attach the other leg in the same way.

7. Cut a long piece of thread. Then, turn the cowboy over and gently push the thread through both holes at the top of the legs, like this.

8. Knot the thread to make a loop. Then, tie a bead onto the ends of the thread that are hanging down. Pull on the thread to make the cowboy 'dance'.

Stallion stampede

Use a medium-sized round coin to draw the horse's cheek.

1. Draw around a coin on thick paper for a horse's cheek. Add ears and a nose. Then, draw a curve for the neck and back, and a circle for the rump.

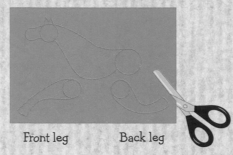

Front leg   Back leg

2. Draw a curve for the chest and neck. Then, make circles for the tops of the legs by drawing around the coin. Add long, curved legs, then cut everything out.

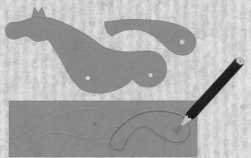

Mark where the holes are.

3. Punch two holes at either end of the body and in the tops of the legs. Then, draw around the legs to make a second pair and cut them out.

Move the horse's legs into different positions to make it look like it is galloping.

Hold the strip near the top as you flatten it.

4. To make hinges, cut two strips that fit through the punched holes. Fold one strip into a loop. Then, push the top of the loop down to flatten it, like this.

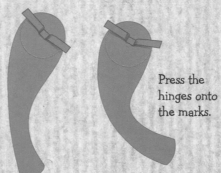

Press the hinges onto the marks.

5. Fold the other hinge in the same way. Dab white glue onto the flattened part of the hinges and press them onto the top of the second pair of legs.

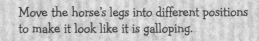

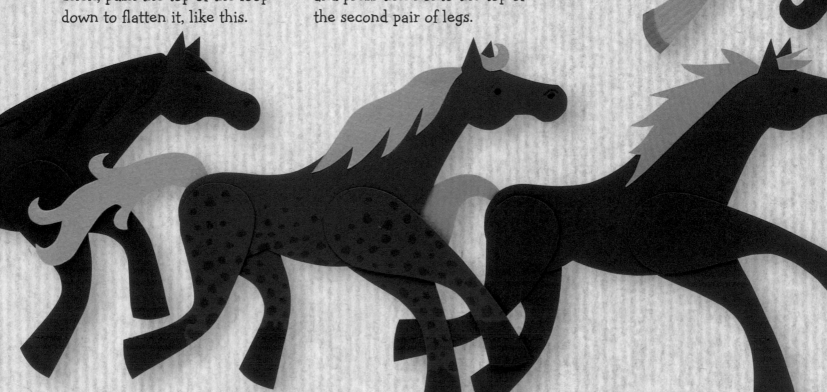

This is the back of the horse.

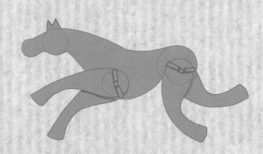

6. Lay the front leg with the hinge flat and slot the hole on the front of the body onto the hinge. Then, slot the other front leg on top of the hinge, like this.

7. Fold out the ends of the hinge and press them down to hold the leg in place. Then, attach the horse's back legs to the body in the same way.

8. Cut out a mane and tail from paper and glue them onto the horse. Then, use a brown felt-tip pen to draw the horse's face and fill in the hooves.

You could make a whole herd of stampeding horses.

Use a felt-tip pen to draw spots and patches on the horses.

Try making cowboy hat and horseshoe stencils, like the ones used to make the paper below.

Howdy Billy the Kid!

Please come to my mighty fine cowboy party on Saturday. Don't forget your horse!

From Sam the Sheriff

You could decorate wrapping paper, envelopes and gift tags, too.

Wild West paper

Cut through both layers.

1. To make a stencil, fold a piece of thick paper in half. Draw half a cactus, like this, against the fold. Then, hold the layers together and cut along the lines.

2. To print the cactus, open out the stencil and lay it at the top of a piece of paper. Then, pour thick green paint onto an old plate and spread it out a little.

3. Dip a sponge into the paint. Then, hold down the stencil and dab paint all over the shape of the cactus. Lift it off the paper and leave the paint to dry.

Series Editor: Fiona Watt • Photographic manipulation by John Russell.
First published in 2008 by Usborne Publishing Ltd., Usborne House, 83-85 Saffron Hill, London, EC1N 8RT. www.usborne.com